anythink

D0768660

NO LONGER PROPERTY OF
ANYTHINK LIBRARIES/
RANGEVIEW LIBRARY DISTRICT

RECIPES OF THE CIVIL WAR

By Amy B. Rogers

KidHaven PUBLISHING

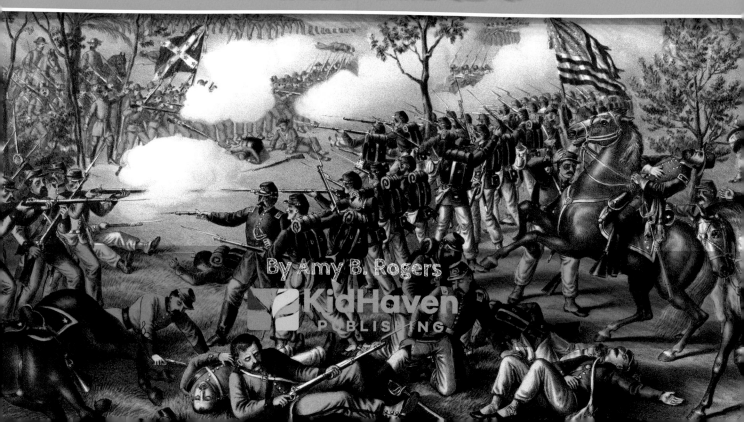

Published in 2017 by
KidHaven Publishing, an Imprint of Greenhaven Publishing, LLC
353 3rd Avenue
Suite 255
New York, NY 10010

Copyright © 2017 KidHaven Publishing, an Imprint of Greenhaven Publishing, LLC.

All rights reserved. No part of this book may be reproduced in any form without permission in writing from the publisher, except by a reviewer.

Designer: Andrea Davison-Bartolotta
Editor: Katie Kawa

Photo credits: Cover, p. 1 (top) Symonenko Viktoriia/Shutterstock.com; cover, p. 1 (bottom) John Parrot/Stocktrek Images/Getty Images; back cover, pp. 2, 3, 7, 9, 17, 19, 22–24 (wood texture) Maya Kruchankova/Shutterstock.com; p. 4 Joseph Sohm/Shutterstock.com; pp. 5, 6, 10, 14, 15, 21 courtesy of the Library of Congress; pp. 7, 9, 17, 19 (notebook) BrAt82/Shutterstock.com; p. 7 (hoecakes) Glenn Price/Shutterstock.com; p. 8 Ekaterina_Minaeva/ Shutterstock.com; p. 9 (bottom) Mariusz S. Jurgielewicz/Shutterstock.com; p. 9 (top) Robert F. Leahy/ Shutterstock.com; pp. 11, 13 Buyenlarge/Archive Photos/Getty Images; p. 16 Tria Giovan/Getty Images; p. 17 (top) Strannik_fox/Shutterstock.com; p. 17 (bottom) paulista/Shutterstock.com; p. 18 Fotosearch/Archive Photos/Getty Images; p. 19 (pie) Lili Blankenhship/Shutterstock.com; p. 20 Morgan Riley/Wikimedia Commons.

Library of Congress Cataloging-in-Publication Data

Names: Rogers, Amy B., author.
Title: Recipes of the Civil War / Amy B. Rogers.
Description: New York : KidHaven Publishing, 2017. | Series: Cooking your way through American history | Includes index.
Identifiers: LCCN 2016036213 (print) | LCCN 2016036619 (ebook) | ISBN 9781534520882 (pbk.) | ISBN 9781534520899 (6 pack) | ISBN 9781534520905 (library bound) | ISBN 9781534520912 (E-book)
Subjects: LCSH: Cooking, American–History–Juvenile literature. | United States–History–Civil War, 1861-1865–Juvenile literature.
Classification: LCC TX715 .R724 2017 (print) | LCC TX715 (ebook) | DDC 641.5973–dc23
LC record available at https://lccn.loc.gov/2016036213

Printed in the United States of America

CPSIA compliance information: Batch #CW17KL: For further information contact Greenhaven Publishing LLC, New York, New York at 1-844-317-7404.

Please visit our website, www.greenhavenpublishing.com. For a free color catalog of all our high-quality books, call toll free 1-844-317-7404 or fax 1-844-317-7405.

CONTENTS

AMERICA SPLITS IN TWO

The American Civil War was one of the most difficult periods in the history of the United States. This war was fought between people in the North, which was sometimes called the Union, and the South, which was sometimes called the Confederacy. This war lasted from 1861 to 1865, and those four years were hard times for people living in the United States.

It wasn't easy being a kid during the Civil War. Sarah was eight years old when the war began on April 12, 1861. She lived with her family on a large farm called a plantation in South Carolina. Until the Civil War, most people in the South had more than enough food to eat. However, that changed during the war. Sarah often had to go without many foods she loved to eat.

plantation

The Civil War affected life all over the United States, but it had the biggest impact on life for Southerners such as Sarah and her family.

SLAVERY IN THE SOUTH

Sarah's family was one of many in the South who owned plantations. On some plantations, people grew food crops, such as rice. Many plantation owners grew cotton and tobacco because these crops could be sold for a lot of money. They were often sold to people in the North and in other countries.

Many plantation owners used slave labor. The slaves were taken from their homes in Africa and forced to move to the United States. There, they often worked in the fields on plantations, and they weren't paid for their work. They and their children were treated as property and not as people. The slaves who lived and worked on Sarah's plantation cooked with whatever **ingredients** they were given. They often made a kind of bread called hoecake.

slave working on a plantation

hoecakes

Ingredients:
½ cup cornmeal
¼ teaspoon salt
1½ teaspoons vegetable oil
½ cup boiling water

Directions:
- Preheat the oven to 375° Fahrenheit (F).
- Mix cornmeal and salt in a small bowl.
- Add the vegetable oil and ¼ cup of the boiling water, and stir well.
- Keep adding more water until the dough is thick and you can work it with your hands.
- Oil the surface of a small cookie sheet with another ½ teaspoon of vegetable oil.
- Shape the dough by hand into two flat, round patties. Place them on the cookie sheet, and put them in the oven.
- Bake the hoecakes for 25 minutes or until they're brown.
- Serve with butter, jam, or anything else you like on bread. This serves two people.

Hoecakes were cooked by slaves on a tool called a hoe over a small fire. You can make hoecakes today using a cookie sheet and an oven. Remember to always ask an adult for help when using the oven, burners on the stove, or sharp kitchen tools.

COOKING ON THE PLANTATION

Plantation owners such as Sarah's family were generally wealthy. They were able to cook and eat large meals every day. These meals often featured baked or boiled meat and vegetables. Sometimes foods were fried in animal fat or butter. Like most people at that time, Sarah's family seasoned their food with salt and pepper.

Sarah loved sweets more than any other kind of food. She helped her mother bake cookies, pies, and cakes. They used spices such as cinnamon, cloves, ginger, and nutmeg in their baking. During the summer, they made jams and jellies. In the fall, after the pecans were harvested, Sarah's mother used them to make praline sauce. Sarah's family ate praline sauce with fruit or cake. Sarah enjoyed making and eating this tasty treat!

pecan tree

praline sauce

Ingredients:
1 cup corn syrup
3 tablespoons brown sugar
2 tablespoons water
½ cup pecans, chopped
½ teaspoon vanilla extract

This recipe for praline sauce tastes great on many desserts. What will you try it on?

Directions:
- Mix the corn syrup, brown sugar, and water in a medium-size pot.
- Cook it over medium heat on the stove, and stir with a spoon.
- When the mixture starts to boil, take the pot off the heat, and stir in the pecans and vanilla extract.
- Serve warm over ice cream, fruit, or cake.

This makes 1½ cups of praline sauce and serves about four people.

THE ROAD TO WAR

Life in the North during this time was different from life on a Southern plantation. Many people in the North didn't support slavery. It was outlawed in many Northern states. The North didn't need slavery for its **economy** the same way the South did. The Northern economy was starting to move away from the farm and toward the factory. People in the North were building machines that worked faster than people ever could.

The South eventually separated from the North and formed its own country, which was called the Confederate States of America. President Abraham Lincoln declared war as he tried to bring the country back together by any means. The Civil War had begun.

Abraham Lincoln

During the Civil War, Sarah's father fought in the Confederate Army. He wanted to **protect** the Southern way of life. Sarah's uncle lived in New York and joined the Union Army. These two men weren't the only family members who fought on different sides of this war.

FOOD BECOMES SCARCE

The Civil War lasted for four long years, and it was an especially hard time for people who lived in the South, such as Sarah's family. Many men in the South **volunteered** to fight for the Confederate Army like Sarah's father did. Few men were left to guard and run cities and plantations in the South. Women such as Sarah's mother had to manage households on their own.

As the war went on, the North stopped shipping food to the South. Union troops later marched through Confederate lands, taking the food and supplies they needed. Confederate soldiers also needed food, and it was difficult to get it to them on the battlefield because roads and railroads were poor in the South. Because of this, many people living in the Confederacy often went hungry.

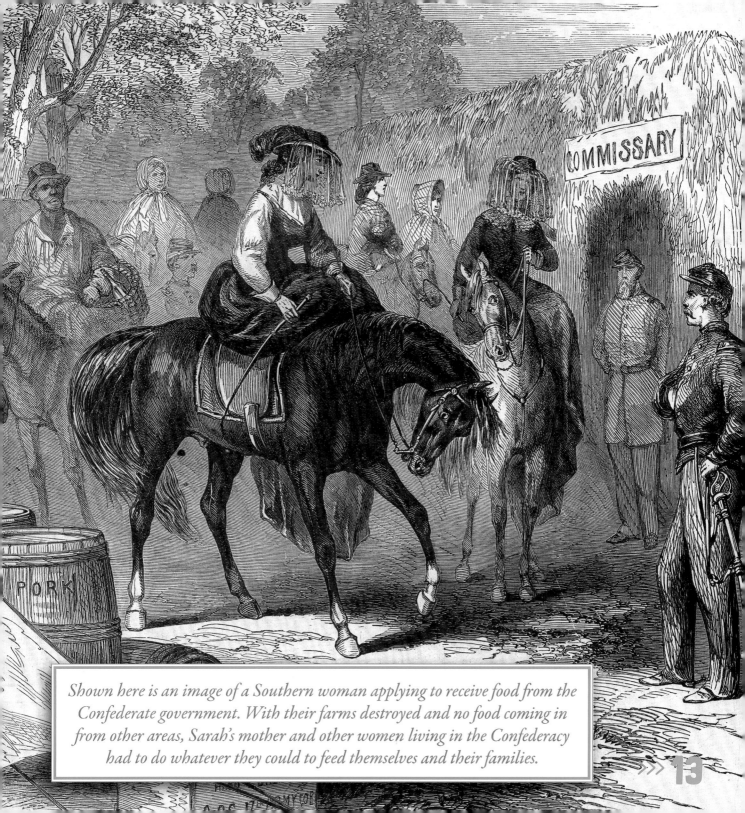

Shown here is an image of a Southern woman applying to receive food from the Confederate government. With their farms destroyed and no food coming in from other areas, Sarah's mother and other women living in the Confederacy had to do whatever they could to feed themselves and their families.

LIFE IN THE NORTH

Sarah's cousin Matthew lived in the North. Unlike people living in the South, Matthew and others in the North often had plenty of food to eat. They had to pay more for it than they did before the war, and sometimes they couldn't buy some of the foods they wanted because of shortages. However, a much smaller number of people went hungry in the North.

Soldiers in the Union Army generally had enough to eat during the war. **Engineers** built roads and railroads to carry supplies, including food, to Union soldiers. The Union also had a steady supply of ice to keep meat cold and fresh while it was being shipped to soldiers. The availability of fresh food for both soldiers and **civilians** greatly helped the Union war effort.

Union soldiers had more food and better food to eat than Confederate soldiers. This helped them stay stronger and able to fight for longer periods of time.

A SOLDIER'S RATIONS

Both Union and Confederate soldiers were given rations, or fixed amounts of food. Men in the Union Army were given meat, beans, peas, rice or **hominy**, coffee or tea, sugar, salt, and pepper, among other foods. Union soldiers also had access to canned milk, as well as canned or dried fruits and vegetables.

The Confederate soldiers ate many of the same things as Union soldiers, including a dry, tasteless cracker called hardtack. However, the Confederate Army had little access to coffee and canned goods because of Union **blockades**. Confederate soldiers, including Sarah's father, were also given less meat than soldiers serving in the Union Army. Cornmeal, which is a kind of flour made from corn, was an important part of their rations.

hardtack

16

salt pork in cornmeal coat

Ingredients:
½ pound salt pork
¼ cup cornmeal
½ cup vegetable oil

Directions:
- Ask an adult to help you cut the skin off the salt pork. Then, cut the salt pork into thick slices.
- Put the slices into a small pot, and cover them with water. Heat the pot on the stove on medium heat until the water starts to boil.
- Turn the heat off, and let the salt pork sit in the hot water for five minutes. Then, drain the water.
- When the salt pork cools, spread the cornmeal on a large plate. Dip the salt pork slices into the cornmeal, coating the slices on both sides. Shake off the extra cornmeal.
- Heat the vegetable oil on the stove in a heavy pan on medium heat. When the oil is hot, gently slip the coated salt pork slices into the oil. Brown them on both sides for about five minutes on each side.

This serves four to five people.

salt pork

*Civil War soldiers often cooked salt pork, which is pork that has been **preserved** using salt. You can cook salt pork with just a few basic ingredients.*

cornmeal

HUNGER IN THE SOUTH

Food shortages had become common in the South by the end of the Civil War. Like many people, Sarah and her mother didn't have enough food to eat and often went hungry. They and their slaves only ate one meal each day. Basic ingredients, such as flour and cornmeal, were expensive. Coffee and sugar weren't available at all.

It was hard to keep meat from spoiling because the trains that brought ice to the South had stopped running. There also wasn't enough salt to preserve meat. By 1863, there was so little food that Sarah's mother and many other Southern women started food **riots**—sometimes called bread riots—to try to get the government's attention. However, the government couldn't do much, even as the people in the South starved.

Richmond Bread Riot

sweet potato pie

Ingredients:

1 pound sweet potatoes
2 eggs
1¼ cups milk
¾ cup brown sugar
1 teaspoon salt
1 teaspoon cinnamon
½ teaspoon nutmeg
3 tablespoons butter, melted
1 9-inch pie crust

Directions:

- Preheat the oven to 425° F.
- Peel, wash, and cut the sweet potatoes into 1-inch pieces.
- Put enough water in a medium-size pot to cover the sweet potatoes, and add ½ teaspoon salt.
- Bring the water to a boil, then turn the heat to low. Cover the pot, and let the sweet potatoes simmer for 20 minutes until they're soft.
- Drain the water, and mash the sweet potatoes in a large bowl.
- Beat the eggs with a fork in a small bowl. Add the eggs, milk, brown sugar, other ½ teaspoon of salt, cinnamon, nutmeg, and melted butter to the sweet potatoes. Mix well.
- Pour the mixture into the pie crust.
- Bake the pie at 425° F for 10 minutes. Then, turn the heat down to 300° F and bake for another 50 minutes.

This serves six to eight people.

Sweet potato pie was one of the foods Sarah missed the most during the war. You can make your own pie using this recipe!

REBUILDING THE SOUTH

The Civil War ended in 1865. Work then began on bringing the divided nation back together. Once slavery was officially **abolished**, some men and women who'd once been slaves moved north to find work. Others stayed in the South.

Southerners struggled after the war. People from both the North and South worked to rebuild this part of the country. That included helping people in the South get food. Sarah's mother stocked her kitchen with different kinds of canned food. This method of preserving food—along with freezing or cooling it with ice—became more common following the Civil War. Sarah and her family were then able to keep food from spoiling for a longer period of time, which was a huge help in the hard years after the war.

advertisement for canned condensed milk

People worked hard after the Civil War to rebuild cities in the South, including Atlanta, Georgia, which is shown here. This period in American history is known as Reconstruction.

GLOSSARY

abolish: To officially end or stop something.

blockade: The cutting off of an area with troops or warships to stop the coming in or going out of people or supplies.

civilian: A person not on active duty in the military.

economy: The process or system by which goods and services are produced, sold, and bought in an area.

engineer: Someone who uses science and math to plan and build machines.

hominy: A food made from dried corn.

ingredient: One of the things used to make a food.

preserve: To keep food from spoiling.

protect: To keep safe.

riot: A violent public disturbance by a group of people.

volunteer: To choose to do something without being forced to do it.

FOR MORE INFORMATION

WEBSITES

Civil War Cooking: What the Union Soldiers Ate

www.pbs.org/food/the-history-kitchen/civil-war-cooking-what-the-union-soldiers-ate/

Discover the story behind how the Union Army was fed, and make your own Civil War beef stew!

"Food From North and South"

www.nytimes.com/2011/09/21/nyregion/recipes-adapted-from-cookbooks-of-the-civil-war-era.html?_r=0

This article features several additional Civil War recipes for making foods such as beef jerky and "Confederate ketchup."

Richmond Bread Riot

www.encyclopediavirginia.org/bread_riot_richmond#start_entry

The Virginia Foundation for the Humanities outlines the most important information about the Richmond Bread Riot of 1863.

BOOKS

Halls, Kelly Milner. *Life During the Civil War.* Minneapolis, MN: Core Library, 2015.

Lanser, Amanda. *The Civil War by the Numbers.* North Mankato, MN: Capstone Press, 2016.

Machajewski, Sarah. *A Kid's Life During the American Civil War.* New York, NY: PowerKids Press, 2015.

Publisher's note to educators and parents: Our editors have carefully reviewed these websites to ensure that they are suitable for students. Many websites change frequently, however, and we cannot guarantee that a site's future contents will continue to meet our high standards of quality and educational value. Be advised that students should be closely supervised whenever they access the Internet.

INDEX